T3-BVW-541

Salad Garnishes

Nita Mehta's
Vegetarian
SaladS

100% TRIED & TESTED RECIPES

Nita Mehta

B.Sc. (Home Science), M.Sc. (Food and Nutrition) Gold Medalist

Tanya Mehta

SNAB
PUBLISHERS PVT LTD

Vegetarian

Nita Mehta's
Vegetarian
SaladS

© Copyright 2004-2007 **SNAB** Publishers Pvt Ltd

3rd Print 2007
ISBN 978-81-7869-083-4

Food Styling and Photography: **SNAB**

Layout and laser typesetting :

National Information
Technology Academy
3A/3, Asaf Ali Road
New Delhi-110002
N.I.T.A. ☎ 23252948

Contributing Writers :
Anurag Mehta
Subhash Mehta

Editorial & Proofreading :
Stephens Chako
Sangeeta

Distributed by :
THE VARIETY BOOK DEPOT
A.V.G. Bhavan, M 3 Con Circus,
New Delhi - 110 001
Tel : 23417175, 23412567; Fax : 23415335
Email: varietybookdepot@rediffmail.com

Printed by :
PARAS OFFSET

Published by :

SNAB
Publishers Pvt. Ltd.
3A/3 Asaf Ali Road,
New Delhi - 110002
Tel: 23252948, 23250091
Telefax:91-11-23250091

Editorial and Marketing office:
E-159, Greater Kailash-II, N.Delhi-48
Fax: 91-11-29225218, 29229558
Tel: 91-11-29214011, 29218727, 29218574
E-Mail: nitamehta@email.com
nitamehta@nitamehta.com
*Website:*http://www.nitamehta.com
Website: http://www.snabindia.com

Rs. 89/-

Introduction

*S*alads should be crisp, colourful, refreshing and delicious. There are no hard and fast rules about the ingredients that should go into a salad. Select salad ingredients to lend colour to the table, but above all let them blend and help to balance the rest of the menu. Salads can be served as an appetizer, a dinner accompaniment or as a main course. A frosty fruit salad can be had as a dessert too.

Ready made mayonnaise, even eggless ones are easily available today. Although the recipe for making mayonnaise is given at the end of the book, keeping a bottle of ready made one is a good idea. It has a longer shelf life than the home made one and is very handy at times. Similarly it is good to stock ready made salsa and mustard paste too. Tetra packs of fresh cream also have a longer shelf life than the fresh dairy cream. Salads add roughage and nutrition to your meals, turning an ordinary meal into a healthy one.

Nita Mehta

ABOUT THE RECIPES

WHAT'S IN A CUP?

INDIAN CUP
1 teacup = 200 ml liquid
AMERICAN CUP
1 cup = 240 ml liquid (8 oz.)
The recipes in this book were tested with the Indian teacup which holds 200 ml liquid.

Contents

Pasta, Rice & Noodle Salad   68

Salad Garnishes

See colour pictures of all the garnishes on page 2

Spring Onion Flowers: Cut off about ¼ inch piece from the white bulb end and leaving 3" from the bulb, cut off the greens. Slice the bulb thinly lengthwise till the end of the bulb. Now make similar cuts at right angles. Similarly for a green side, cut the green leaves almost till the stem end to get thin strips. Place in iced water for some time until it opens up like a flower. A good garnish for a Chinese salad!

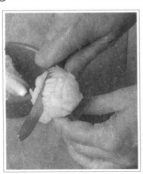  

Fruit Bowls: Make a deep 'V' cut in the centre of watermelon. To do this, make about 2" slant cut first & then another one a little away from the first one, but which meets at the bottom forming a 'V'. Continue cutting in the same way all around the melon to get a VVVV edge when the two pieces are separated. When cutting, keep the knife tilted and go deep inside. Separate the two pieces. Make the piece hollow, keeping a little red border showing. Cover the empty bowl with a plastic wrap and refrigerate. Fill salad in it at serving time. You may add some chopped watermelon pieces to the salad. Do not add too much watermelon to the salad or you may end up serving a fruit salad.

Carrot and Radish (mooli) Tuberoses: Take a slender carrot or radish. Peel and wash it. Make a sharp angled cut, at about a height of 1½", about ½"

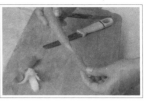

downwards and inwards. Make 2 similar cuts from the remaining sides - all the cuts should meet at the end. Hold the top of the carrot with one hand, and the base with the other. Twist the lower portion to break off the top portion. You will have a tuberose in one hand and the remaining part of the carrot in the other. Trim the left over carrot to get a pointed end. Make more flowers from the left over carrot. Keep them in ice-cold water for upto 3-4 days without getting spoilt. You can make such flowers with white radish (mooli) also. Goes well with light French dressing salads.

Coloured Capsicum Baskets: Slice the top of a coloured (yellow, red or green capsicum). Make ½" deep V cuts all around the edge to get a 'VVVV' edge. Leave the bunch of seeds in it as they are. Place on the side of a large platter of salad.

Tomato Rose: Take a very firm red tomato. Beginning at stem end, start cutting the skin as though you were peeling it in a long strip. The strip should be as long as possible, as thin as possible and about ½" to 1" wide. See that you keep changing the width of the strip as you go on peeling it. Do not let the strip be

uniform in width. The rose looks more natural if the strip is cut uneven. If while peeling, it breaks, keep the broken part aside for use later on and continue cutting the peel. Now start rolling up the long strip firmly. Place it on the salad. Place the other parts of the strip around the rolled peel. The tomato strip should now look like a real rose. Looks good on a sour cream or mayonnaise dressing salad.

Chilli Flower: Choose a slightly thick chilli. Cut into half starting from the tip almost till the end, leaving ½" from stem end. Cut each half with a scissor into many thin strips, keeping all intact at base. Put it in chilled water for 4-5 hours in the fridge. It opens up to a flower. Goes well with a spicy Thai salad!

Salad Tips

FOR SUCCESS IN SALAD MAKING...

- Use fresh crisp ingredients.
- Wash vegetables carefully in running water if possible.
- Pat dry leafy vegetables and other vegetables on a clean kitchen towel for complete removal of moisture after washing.
- Always tear lettuce apart, never cut with a knife.
- Add colour and variety by using tomatoes, grated or diced carrots, colourful fruits and nuts.
- Be careful about the texture. Do not use too soft and mushy fruits and vegetables. If the tomatoes are soft, it is a good idea to deseed them.
- Thorough chilling is a secret to success in salad. Chill the salad bowl or plate as well as the ingredients in a refrigerator.

- Dressing should be poured at the time of serving to maintain the crispness of the greens. Toss the salad gently at the last moment. Use a large bowl and salad tongs or forks to toss the salad.
- Use of appropriate dressing makes all the difference. Dressing is the key to success. Too much dressing makes the salad limp and runny. On the other hand too little dressing makes the salad taste dry. The dressing should be just enough to coat the vegetables/meat.
- Different flavouring can be added to the dressing, like fresh herbs (mint, parsley, dill, basil); dried herbs, freshly crushed pepper, mustard and chilli flakes. Make it tangy with lemon juice and lemon rind, pickled onion and jalapenos.
- Finally, bring eye appeal. Cut your vegetable and fruits in generous chunks or slices. Simple coulourless salad can be improved by simple garnishing of crisp tomato rose or spring onion flower or fruit slices, to make your creation more interesting and attractive.

All Time Favourite Salads

Herbed Croutons as Topping for Salads

A common topping which can be used for topping salad. It surely lends a crunch as well as adds up to the taste of any salads!

Cut 1 day old bread into tiny cubes, about ¼" cubes. Heat oil in a kadhai. Reduce heat. Add 1 cube of bread. If it comes up to the surface and turns golden in a few seconds, the oil is ready. Add bread cubes to the hot oil and remove from oil immediately when they start to change colour, within 1 minute or they will turn extra brown. Immediately sprinkle the hot fried croutons with ¼ tsp pepper or oregano or basil or mixed herbs and a pinch of salt.

Corn in Cup

Serves 6-8   Picture on inside front cover

1½ cups tinned corn kernels (see note)
2 tbsp butter
½ tsp salt, ½ tsp chaat masala
½ tsp red chilli flakes or ¼ tsp red chilli powder
1½ tbsp lemon juice or to taste

1. Melt butter in a kadhai. Add tinned corn, salt, chaat masala and red chilli flakes or powder. Stir for 2 minutes. Add lemon juice, mix well and remove from fire.
2. Serve warm immediately in small plastic cups or regular small cups or glass bowls (katoris).

Note: You can use fresh corn also, but with tinned corn the taste will be much better. When boiling fresh corn, do not add salt while boiling as this will harden corn kernels. Add sugar and haldi to the water and boil corn in it for 5 minutes. Add salt after removing from fire. Let corn be in hot salted water for 10 more minutes & then strain.

Mixed Capsicum Salad

*A very colourful and decorative salad. In the absence of coloured capsicums,
use the same quantity of green capsicums.*

Picture on facing page   *Serves 5*

½ cup finely chopped red capsicum
½ cup finely chopped yellow capsicum
½ cup finely chopped green capsicum
2 spring onions finely chopped along with the green part (1 cup)
½ cup finely chopped onion
3 tbsp fresh cilantro/green coriander - finely chopped
1 tbsp finely chopped pickled jalapenos or 1 tsp chopped green chillies
¾ tsp salt, 2-3 tbsp lemon juice
3 tbsp olive oil
¼ tsp pepper, 1 tsp tomato ketchup

1. Chop all ingredients very finely. Put all the ingredients of the salad in a bowl and mix well. Chill in the fridge for 1-2 hours before serving.
2. Mix well once before serving. Serve chilled with any snack or by itself.

Lotus Stem & Guava Salad

Lotus stem (bhein) can be very troublesome at times because of the dirt stuck inside the holes. To avoid the cleaning hassle, buy lotus stem which is closed at both ends. The closed ends prevent the dirt going inside the stem and you get clean white slices when you cut it.

Serves 47   Picture on opposite page

200-250 gm bhein or kamal kakri (lotus stem) - peel, cut into thin diagonal slices
(about 2 cups)
3-4 tbsp cornflour
oil for frying
1 white amrood (guava)
1 pink amrood (guava)

DRESSING
2 tbsp olive oil, 1 tbsp lemon juice
1 tsp chaat masala
½ tsp salt, ¼ tsp sugar
¼ tsp red chilli powder

Contd...

1 green chilli - deseeded and sliced into thin long pieces
½ tbsp ginger - cut into juliennes or thin match stick like pieces

1. Heat oil for deep frying in a kadhai.
2. Cut lotus stem into ¼" thin diagonal slices and pat dry with a cloth.
3. Sprinkle cornflour, a pinch of salt and a pinch of pepper over the lotus stem (kamal kakri). Mix well to coat the slices.
4. Deep fry till crisp. Remove on paper.
5. Cut apple and amrood with the peel into cubes.
6. Put all ingredients of the dressing in a big bowl. Mix well with a fork.
7. Add lotus stem and amrood. Mix gently. Serve garnished with green chilli and g i n g e r matchsticks.

Greek Salad

Serves 4-6

1½ cups shredded red cabbage
1 cup ice berg lettuce - torn into small pieces
200 gm paneer - cut into 1" cubes, 8-10 green or black olives - cut each into 2
1 tomato - deseeded and thinly sliced

DRESSING

4 tbsp cream, 4 tbsp curd, 1 tbsp lemon juice
1 tbsp mustard paste, ½ tsp salt ¼ tsp pepper

TO GARNISH

1 slice bread cubes - fried to make croutons (see page 16)
2 tbsp roasted peanuts (moongphali)

1. In a bowl place cabbage, lettuce, paneer, olives and tomatoes. Mix.
2. Gently mix all ingredients of dressing and pour over the salad. Mix well. Chill in the fridge till serving time.
3. Take out 15 minutes before serving from fridge, mix gently. Serve topped with fried bread croutons and peanuts.

Bread Croutons

23

Thai Raw Mango Salad

A very unusual and quick salad. Goes well with an Indian meal. It is generally eaten like a chutney, so make a small bowl for 4-6 people.

Picture on backcover   *Serves 6-8*

3 cups juliennes (match sticks) of raw green, mangoes (3 big mangoes)
½ cup roasted or fried kaju (cashew nuts) or peanuts (moongphali)
1- 2 spring onions (hara pyaz)
OR
½ small onion and ½ capsicum - cut into shreds (thin long strips)
2-3 tbsp mango chutney (you can use home made or ready made)
1-2 dry red chillies - crushed (½ tsp)
1 tsp soya sauce
salt and pepper to taste
3-4 flakes garlic - crushed
1 tsp honey or powdered sugar if needed

1. Cut white bulb of spring onion into rings and greens into 1" diagonal pieces.
2. Peel green mangoes. Cut the side pieces. Cut into thin match sticks or juliennes. Keep aside.
3. Mix all ingredients except cashew nuts and honey in a bowl. Add sugar or honey if mangoes are very sour. Keep covered in the refrigerator for 2-3 hours for the flavour to penetrate.

4. At serving time, top with roasted or fried nuts and mix lightly.

Note: Ready-made mango chutney is available in the market in small bottles.

Crispy Spinach with Feta

Feta cheese resembles Indian paneer. We have added some vinegar to it.

Picture on page 103   *Serves 4-6*

250 gm spinach leaves (2 cups), 1 small cucumber (kheera)
1 onion - cut into 8 pieces and separated
1 large tomato - cut into 4 remove pulp and chop into very small pieces
5-6 leaves of lettuce - tear into small pieces or ½ cup cabbage- chopped

DRESSING
3 tbsp oil, preferably olive oil
1 tsp vinegar, ¾ tsp salt, ½ tsp pepper
½ tsp oregano (dried), 1 tbsp milk

TOPPING (MIX TOGETHER)
½ cup roughly mashed (crumbled) paneer
¼ tsp salt, ¼ tsp pepper, 1 tbsp vinegar

1. Wash spinach leaves. Remove stalk. Pat dry leaves on a clean kitchen towel. Keep aside for 30 minutes.
2. Heat oil in a kadhai, deep fry few leaves at a time. Fry leaves carefully (oil splutters!) in 5 batches till

crisp & dark green. Do not let them turn brown while frying. Drain on paper napkins with a pair of tongs (chimta). Keep aside & not in the fridge but outside, till further use. (Fried leaves turn limp in the fridge!)

3. Remove bitterness of the cucumber. Cut lengthwise into two halves. With the help of a scooper or the back of a teaspoon, remove the seeds from the cucumber by pulling the spoon straight down the length of the cucumber half. This way you get a groove in the cucumber piece.

4. Cut the cucumber into ½" thick, half-moon slices.
5. Put all ingredients of dressing in a big bowl. Mix well with a wire whisk or fork.
6. Except for fried spinach, add all chopped vegetables to bowl. Mix well. Transfer the salad to a serving bowl. Keep salad aside in the fridge to chill.

7. Mix all ingredients of topping in a bowl. Keep aside till serving time.
8. To serve, add fried spinach to the salad, mix gently. Sprinkle topping mixture over the salad. Serve.

Mozzarella with Tomatoes

Picture on facing page   *Serves 4*

3 small, firm, red tomatoes, 100 gm mozzarella (pizza) cheese
6-8 black olives - cut into two halves
a few parsley or basil leaves - dipped in chilled water
DRESSING
2 tbsp balsamic vinegar, 4 tbsp olive oil
2 garlic flakes - chopped very finely, ½ tsp dried oregano
¼ tsp salt and ¼ tsp freshly crushed pepper, or to taste

1. Slice the tomatoes into circles and the cheese into 1" squares of ¼" thickness.
2. In a flat platter, arrange the cheese slices. Top each with a tomato slice. Arrange an olive half and a parsley or basil leaf on the tomato slice.
3. Make the dressing by mixing balsamic vinegar, olive oil, chopped garlic, oregano, salt and pepper with a fork or balloon whisk till well blended.
4. Spoon some dressing on the tomato and cheese slices. Cover with a plastic wrap and keep aside in the refrigerator till serving time.

Italian Sour Cream Salad

Serves 4   *Picture on opposite page*

SOUR CREAM DRESSING

1 cup thick curd - hang for 30 minutes in a muslin cloth
2-3 tbsp grated cheddar cheese (use tin or cubes)
75 gm (½ cup fresh cream)
2 tbsp roasted peanuts (moongphali) - split into two halves or pounded
2 flakes garlic - crushed to a paste
1 tbsp olive oil
½ tsp oregano
1 tsp tomato ketchup, ½ tsp salt, ¼ tsp pepper

OTHER INGREDIENTS

¾ cup carrots - cut into ¼" pieces
½ cup sliced baby corns (round slices) - paper thin slices
¼ cup chopped french beans, 2 tbsp chopped celery stalks
½ cup finely chopped cucumber or shredded capsicum
3 slices tinned pineapple - chopped into small pieces
a few lettuce leaves - torn into 1" pieces

Contd...

GARNISH
some musambi or red or green capsicum rings
a tomato - to make a rose, see page 13

1. Hang curd for 30 minutes in a muslin cloth.
2. Mix all ingredients of the sour cream dressing with a wire whisk till smooth. Keep aside in the fridge.
3. Boil 4-5 cups of water with 1 tsp salt and 1 tsp sugar. Add french beans, carrots and baby corns in boiling water and cook for 1-2 minutes till crisp tender. Do not over boil.

4. When done, drain immediately and refresh by putting in cold water (so as to retain their colour). Strain. Keep in the strainer for 10 minutes.
5. Mix all vegetables and fruit in a large bowl.
6. Add the prepared dressing gradually over the fruit and vegetable mixture, mixing gently. Check salt and pepper. Transfer to a serving dish.

7. Make a border of capsicum or halved musambi slices. Make a tomato rose in the centre. Serve cold.

Warm Mushroom Salad

Serves 4

200 gm button mushroom (fresh) - cut each into 2 pieces
1 large onion - cut into 12 pieces
1 large capsicum - cut into 1" pieces, 1 tbsp oil

DRESSING

2 tbsp oil, 1½ tbsp garlic - chopped, 3 tbsp tomato ketchup, ½ tsp salt
1 tsp jeera (cumin seeds), 1 tsp saboot dhania (coriander seeds)
3 dry red chillies (whole dried) - deseed a little, 2 tbsp milk

1. Wash and pat dry mushrooms. Trim the stem and cut each mushroom into two.
2. For dressing, place all ingredients of dressing in a mixer and blend to a paste.
3. Cut onion and capsicum. Keep all vegetables aside till serving time.
4. To serve, heat 1 tbsp oil in a non stick pan. Add onion, mushrooms & capsicum. Saute on low heat for 2 minutes. Remove from fire to bowl.
5. Pour dressing over the sauteed vegetables. Mix gently. Serve warm or at room temperature.

Pineapple & Potato Salad

Serves 6

4 potatoes - peeled and cut into ¾" cubes
2 cups fresh ripe and yellow pineapple - chopped, (buy one which is yellow)
2 spring onions (hara pyaz)

DRESSING
1½ cups fresh curd - hang for ½ hour in a muslin cloth (mal- mal ka kapda)
¾ tsp salt, ½ tsp pepper, 1 tsp vinegar

TEMPERING/TADKA
3 tbsp olive oil, 1 tsp chopped garlic
¾ tsp rai (mustard seeds), ¾ tsp jeera (cumin seeds)
3 tbsp melon seeds (magaz) or chopped almonds

TOPPING
3 tbsp mint leaves (poodina) - chopped

1. Hang curd in a muslin cloth for ½ hour.
2. Cut spring onions into slices up to the greens (1 cup).
3. Peel the potatoes and cut into ¾" pieces.
4. Boil 6 cups of water with 1 tsp salt. Add the potatoes and boil for about 20 minutes till tender but firm. Check with a knife to see that they are cooked.
5. Mix the potatoes with pineapple and spring onions.
6. Put the hung curd in a big bowl and add salt, pepper and vinegar. Mix well with a fork or wire whisk.
7. Add the potato- vegetable mixture to the curd. Mix well. Transfer to a serving bowl.
8. Heat olive oil in a small pan on very low heat. Add garlic, rai and jeera. Cook till jeera turns golden. Add magaz or almonds. Stir.
9. Pour this immediately over the potato salad. Chill in the fridge till serving time.
10 At the time of serving top the salad with chopped mint leaves. Serve.

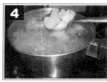

Steamed Sesame Sticks

Taste very good as an appetizer before the main meal and also with the meal. Serve it with a cheesy dip.

Serves 4

4 carrots - peeled & cut into thick match sticks (2 cups)
1 small cucumber (kheera) - cut into thick match sticks without peeling (1½ cups)
2 tbsp sesame seeds (til)

DRESSING (MIX TOGETHER WITH A WIRE WHISK)
2 tbsp olive oil
2 tbsp vinegar
2 tbsp ready-made orange juice
½ tsp salt
½ tsp pepper

1. Cut carrot and cucumber into matchsticks.
2. Put 4 cups of water in a pan and bring to a boil. Place a colander (a big steel strainer with big holes) on the pan. Put the carrot pieces in the colander. Cover colander with a lid and steam the carrots for 2 minutes.
3. Uncover and add the cucumber. Cover and steam further for 1 minute.
4. Remove to a bowl. Pour the dressing over the vegetable sticks and mix well. Keep covered in the fridge till serving time.
5. To serve, toast the sesame seeds on a tawa for 2 minutes on low heat till golden.
6. Pick up the vegetable sticks from the bowl and place in a flat platter. Sprinkle sesame seeds and serve.

wire whisk

colander

Red Bean & Chickpea Salad

A delicious, crunchy salad!

Picture on facing page   *Serves 8-10*

½ cup rajmah (red kidney beans)
½ cup saffed/kabuli channas (chickpeas)
1 cup grapes (black or green) or 1 cup peeled pieces of orange
1 small capsicum - thinly sliced
1 onion - thinly sliced
2 tomatoes - deseeded and thinly sliced

DRESSING
4 tbsp mango chutney (use ready-made or home made)
4 tbsp olive oil
1 tbsp honey
¼ cup chopped coriander leaves
1 tbsp crushed garlic
2 green chillies - chopped

1. Soak rajmah and channa for 2 hours in hot water.
2. Put rajmah, channa, 1 cup water and ½ tsp salt in a pressure cooker. Pressure cook to give 1 whistle. Reduce heat and cook for 4-5 minutes. Do not cook longer. Remove from fire. Let the pressure drop by itself. Drain.
3. Place boiled rajmah, channa, grapes or orange, capsicum, onion and tomatoes in a bowl. Mix well.
4. Place all the ingredients of the dressing in a mixer and blend to a smooth puree.
5. Pour the dressing over the salad and mix well. Chill for 1 hour and serve chilled.

◄ *Kimchi Salad : Recipe on page 42*

Kimchi Salad

The popular Chinese salad. It is always served at the start of a Chinese meal in most Chinese restaurants. The cabbage is almost raw (just blanched) with a spicy, sweet and sour dressing.

Picture on page 40   *Serves 4*

½ of a medium cabbage (300 gms), 1 tbsp ginger match sticks

SYRUP
¼ cup sugar, ¼ cup water
1 tsp salt, ¼ tsp red chilli flakes, ¼ tsp pepper
1 tsp crushed garlic, 2 tbsp vinegar

ADD LATER
½ tsp coarse salt (sendha namak), ¼ tsp white pepper
1 tsp soya sauce, 1 tbsp tomato ketchup, 1 tsp red chilli sauce

1. Cut cabbage into 1" square pieces. Put in a big bowl. Add ginger match sticks also.
2. Boil ¼ cup of water with ¼ cup sugar. Simmer for 2 minutes. Add salt, pepper, red chilli flakes, garlic and vinegar. Remove from fire immediately and pour the hot syrup on the cabbage in the bowl. Cover with a lid, pressing the cabbage. Keep aside for 2 hours.

3. Strain the cabbage. Leave it in the strainer for 15 minutes for the syrup to drain out completely.
4. Add all the other ingredients to the cabbage and toss lightly so that the sauces coat the cabbage. Serve at room temperature.

Potato, Apple & Celery Salad

Serves 5-6

12 baby potatoes, choose really tiny ones or 2 big potatoes
3 large, red apples (delicious) - cut into ½" cubes without peeling
3-4 stalks celery - cut into ¼-½" slices (½ cup)
3-4 tbsp chopped walnuts (akhrot)
1 tbsp lemon juice
1 tbsp oil
salt & pepper to taste
¾ cup ready-made mayonnaise (eggless mayonnaise is available in bottles)

GARNISH
2-3 lettuce leaves

1. Wash and peel baby potatoes. In the
    absence of baby potatoes, make balls of
    a big potato with the help of a melon
    scooper.

2. Place potatoes in a sauce pan with 4-5 cups water and 2 tsp salt. Bring to a boil. Cover and cook on low heat for 10 minutes, till potatoes turn soft. Remove from fire and strain. Transfer to a mixing bowl.

3. Chop the celery stem into ¼-½" pieces (½ cup) as shown in picture. Keep aside (only stem is used).

4. Cut the unpeeled apples into ½" cubes and mix with the potatoes in the bowl.

5. Add 1 tbsp oil and lemon juice immediately, so that the apples do not discolour.

6. Add chopped celery stalks, salt and pepper and toss gently to mix the salad well. Cover with a cling film (plastic wrap) and chill covered for 1-2 hours or till serving time.

7. Before serving, add the walnuts and pour the mayonnaise. Mix gently. Check seasoning.

8. To serve, fill half bowl with salad. Arrange 2-3 lettuce leaves on a side. Fill the bowl with the left over salad. Serve cold.

Crispy Okra & Grape Salad

A very refreshing salad with a Mediterranean dressing of chick-peas flavoured with fresh herbs like mint and fenugreek. When fresh fenugreek leaves are unavailable, use half the quantity of dried fenugreek (kasoori methi).

Serves 4-6

500 gm bhindi (okra) - cut into diagonal slices
2 tbsp cornflour, oil for frying
1 potato - boiled, peeled and cut into small cubes
1 cup green and 1 cup black grapes - halved into 2 pieces

DRESSING
2 tbsp oil
3 tbsp kabuli/saffed channas (chickpeas) - soaked in warm water for 3 hours or more
2 tbsp poodina (mint leaves)
¼ cup fresh methi leaves (fenugreek leaves)
2 tbsp lemon juice, 2 tsp sugar, ½ tsp salt to taste
1 tsp red chilli flakes
¼ cup curd

1. Soak channas overnight in tap water or for 2-3 hours in warm water. Measure ¼ cup of soaked channas.

2. Grind ¼ cup soaked channas alongwith all the other ingredients of the dressing to a smooth sauce. Keep aside.

3. Wash and pat dry bhindi.

4. Cut bhindi into diagonal slices.

5. Sprinkle dry cornflour over it. Mix well.

6. Heat oil in a kadhai. Fry the bhindi on medium flame till crisp. Do not make it brown by frying in very hot oil. Remove from oil on paper napkins. Let it cool down to room temperature.

7. At serving time, place bhindi, potatoes and grapes in a serving bowl. Sprinkle salt and pepper over it. Pour the dressing over the salad & mix well. Check salt and serve immediately at room temperature.

Cole Slaw

The preferred accompaniment to most Continental food.

Serves 4-6

2 cups shredded green cabbage
½ cup shredded red cabbage, if unavailable, take ½ cup more of green cabbage
1 small onion - chopped finely
1 large carrot - grated thickly
2-3 slices pineapple or 1 orange - skinned, peeled and cut into ½" pieces a few
black grapes, optional
¾ cup ready-made mayonnaise, eggless mayonnaise is available in bottles
4 tbsp cream

VINAIGRETTE DRESSING
2 tbsp vinegar, 1 tsp mustard paste or powder
4 tbsp olive oil or any cooking oil
¼ tsp salt, ¼ tsp sugar, ¼ tsp pepper powder

1. Mix all the ingredients of the vinaigrette dressing together in a small bowl. Mix well with a balloon whisk or fork.
2. Remove the hard core of the cabbage and shred very finely with a sharp knife or in a food processor. Use the outer green leaves also as they are very firm and dark in colour.
3. Mix cabbage and onion in a salad bowl. Pour the vinaigrette dressing over and chill covered in the refrigerator for 4-5 hours.
4. After 4-5 hours, drain any vinaigrette dressing at the bottom of the bowl.
5. Add carrot, pineapple or orange and grapes to the salad bowl.
6. Pour mayonnaise and cream over and mix gently.
7. Taste the coleslaw for seasoning and add salt, pepper and mustard according to taste. Serve chilled.

Shredding of Cabbage

To shred cabbage, cut cabbage into 4 pieces. Remove the hard core. Place a flat side of the ¼ head of cabbage on a cutting board. Cut into thin slices with a large sharp knife. Cut slices several times to make smaller pieces.

Pineapple & Sprout Salad

Serves 4

SALAD

1½ cups (250 gm) moong sprouts or mixed sprouts
1½ cups fresh pineapple - chopped into ½-1" pieces
6-8 leaves lettuce
¼ cup vinegar, 1 tsp salt, 1 tsp sugar
1 small onion - thinly sliced
6-8 cherry tomatoes or 1 small tomato - cut into 8 pieces and pulp removed

DRESSING

2 tbsp olive oil, ¼ cup orange juice (fresh or packet)
½ tsp sugar if using fresh juice
1 tbsp vinegar or 2 tbsp lemon juice, ½ tsp freshly ground pepper
½ tsp mustard paste or powder, ½ tsp salt

GARNISH

a few lettuce leaves - dipped in ice water for 15-20 minutes to become crisp

1. Dip the lettuce leaves in 2 cups ice cold water mixed with vinegar, salt sugar for 15-20 minutes for the leaves to become crisp
2. Boil 2 cups water with 1 tsp salt, 1 tsp sugar and ¼ cup vinegar. Add sprouts to boiling water. After the boil returns, keep it boiling for 1 minute. Remove from fire. Drain. Refresh in cold water. Leave the sprouts in the strainer for a while so as to drain out all the water.
3. Mix pineapple and onion in a bowl. Add the sprouts too.
4. Combine all the dressing ingredients in a bottle and shake well or blend in a mixer.
5. Pour over the salad and chill.
6. At serving time, pat dry the lettuce leaves on a clean kitchen towel. Tear a few lettuce leaves into two pieces and mix with the salad.
7. Line a salad bowl with crisp whole lettuce leaves. Place the prepared salad in the bowl and serve.

Note: Instead of moong sprouts, a mixture of any of these or of all these may be used according to your preference - cheese cut into small strips or cubes, paneer cubes, some boiled rice, apple cubes, cucumber, capsicum, orange segments, cherry and dried apricots.

Salad Nicoise

The French call it NEE- SWAHS! Salad tossed in mustard vinaigrette dressing.

Picture on page 1   *Serves 3-4*

1 tomato - cut into 8 pieces or 8 cherry tomatoes
1 potato - boiled and cut into 8 slices lengthwise
4-6 french beans - threaded and boiled keep whole
6-8 round slices of cucumber (kheera)
1 tbsp capers, optional
6 black or green olives
4-5 lettuce leaves - roughly torn and dipped in chilled water
2 tbsp chopped fresh herbs - mint or parsley or coriander

CREAMY HONEY MUSTARD VINAIGRETTE
1½ tbsp vinegar, 6-7 tbsp olive oil
1 tsp powdered sugar, 2 tsp mustard paste
½ tsp salt & ¼ tsp pepper, or to taste
2 tbsp fresh cream
1 tsp honey

1. For the honey mustard vinaigrette dressing, put all ingredients, except cream into a glass or a small mixer. Mix well with a whisk or churn well in a mixer. Mix until the dressing has lightly emulsified. Store, covered, in the refrigerator. Before using, bring the jar to room temperature for atleast 30 minutes before the dressing is needed and shake again.

2. Add 2 tbsp chopped fresh herbs such as mint or parsley or coriander for a stronger flavour and shake up in the dressing.

3. At the time of serving, wrap the lettuce leaves in a clean kitchen towel to pat dry the leaves well. Put them at the bottom of the serving bowl.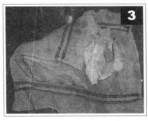

4. Pour 1 tbsp dressing on them.

5. Put green beans, cucumber, potatoes and tomatoes also on the lettuce. Pour the dressing.

6. Top with capers, black olives, parsley. Lightly toss. Serve cold.

Salsa Topped Salad

Picture on cover　　　　　　　*Serves 3-4*

¼ cup curd, a pinch of salt and 1 tsp lemon juice - well beaten together

MIX TOGETHER
½ green capsicum - cut into 1" square pieces
½ red and ½ yellow capsicum - cut into 1" square pieces
1 small onion - sliced thinly
½ cup tinned corn or 1 boiled potato - finely chopped (½ cup)
½ cup chopped paneer (75 gms)
1 tsp salt, ½ tsp pepper, ½ tsp oregano
1 tbsp olive oil, 1 tsp vinegar
3- 4 black olives - sliced

SALSA (GIVES 1 CUP)
5 tomatoes - roasted, 1 tbsp oil
1 onion - chopped finely, 2 green chillies - chopped
2 tbsp chopped coriander
1 tsp vinegar, ½ tsp salt, ¼ tsp pepper, ½ tsp sugar or to taste
1 tbsp tomato sauce

1. For salsa, roast tomatoes by pierceing a tomato with a fork or hold it with a pair of tongs on the flame till the skin turns blackish and charred. Roast all the tomatoes like this. Cool and peel. Do not wash after peeling.
2. Chop 2 tomatoes and puree the other 3 tomatoes in a mixer.
3. Heat 1 tbsp oil, add chopped onion and green chillies. Cook till onion turns soft.
4. Add all the other ingredients and cook for 2 minutes. Do not cook further. Remove from fire. Keep aside in the refrigerator till serving time.
5. Mix all the ingredients of the salad in a bowl. Transfer to a serving bowl. Chill in the fridge till serving time, mix gently again before serving.
6. Pour curd with a spoon over the salad in circles.
7. Top the salad in the center portoin with salsa.
8. Serve extra salsa separately in another bowl along with the salad if someone needs more. Serve chilled.

Russian Salad

Picture on facing page   *Serves 4-6*

1 potato - cut into ½" small pieces
1 tbsp vinegar, 1 tbsp oil
½ cup peas (matar)
2 carrots - diced neatly into small cubes (1½ cups)
8-10 french beans - chopped (½ cup)
½ capsicum - cut into thin long pieces (juliennes)
4-5 slices of pineapple (tinned)
salt and pepper to taste
5-6 crisp lettuce leaves - chill leaves in a bowl of water for 2 hours to turn crisp

DRESSING
¾ cup ready made or home made mayonnaise (see recipe on page 99)
¼ cup fresh cream
1 cube cheese - grated (4 tbsp) or 1 tbsp cheese spread
½ tsp salt, ½ tsp pepper

1. Peel and cut potato into ½" pieces and boil in salted water. Drain, pat dry potatoes with a kitchen towel. Marinate them with oil and vinegar
2. Boil 2 cups water with ½ tsp salt. Add peas. As soon as the boil returns, keep boiling for 2 minutes or till peas are tender. Add the beans and carrots and boil further for 1 minute only. Remove from fire and strain. Add fresh water and strain again. Keep vegetables aside.
3. Mix mayonnaise, cream, cheese spread, salt and pepper. Mix well.
4. Squeeze pineapple slices well to remove excess syrup. Chop finely.
5. Add potato, chopped pineapple, boiled vegetables and capsicum to the mayonnaise. Mix well.
6. Taste and adjust seasonings if needed. Add more pepper if required. Keep aside till serving time.
7. To serve, add a little milk to the salad if it appears extra thick. Arrange lettuce on a flat or a shallow serving platter. Pile the salad in the platter, forming a pyramid (heap). Serve chilled.

Note: The left over tinned pineapple can be stored in a plastic or steel box in the freezer of the refrigerator for 2-3 months.

◁ *Caesar Salad : Recipe on page 60*

Caesar Salad

Picture on page 58   *Serves 3-4*

1 bunch lettuce, preferably iceberg variety
3 slices of white bread - cut into tiny cubes and fried to make croutons (see
recipe on page 16)
6-8 thin slices of cucumber (kheera)
1 tomato - cut into 8 pieces and deseeded
1 cup parmesan or cheddar cheese, Britannia's cubes - shredded

THE CREAMY FRENCH DRESSING
1 tbsp mustard paste
¼ cup olive oil
1 tbsp lemon juice
2 flakes garlic - finely chopped (¾ tsp finely chopped)
¼ cup cream
1 tbsp chopped fresh parsley or 1 tsp dried parsley or 1 tsp chopped coriander
¼ tsp salt and ¼ tsp pepper

TOPPING (OPTIONAL)
1 French bean, a few black olives

1. Wash the lettuce leaves, in plenty of water to remove grit. Keep in ice cold water in a bowl in the fridge till serving time.
2. For bread croutons, remove crusts of bread slices and cut bread into small squares. Heat oil in a frying pan & deep fry over medium heat until they just turn golden. Remove to a paper napkin.
3. Shred cheese into very thin long slices with a potato peeler.
4. To prepare the dressing, combine all the ingredients of the dressing and blend together in a mixer. Keep in the fridge till serving time. If it turns too thick, add 2 tbsp water to make it slightly thinner.
5. At the time of serving the salad, remove lettuce from water and tear into bite sizes pieces with your hands and put on a kitchen towel to absorb any water.
6. Put the leaves in a bowl. Pour some dressing on the leaves.
7. Top the salad leaves with bread croutons and cheese shavings.
8. Arrange the cucumber and tomatoes alternately on the sides to form a border. Pour the prepared creamy French dressing on the sides and in the centre also. Serve topped with a bean in the centre and few olives.

Veggies in Mustard Dressing

Serves 4

MUSTARD DRESSING
½ cup thick curd - beat till smooth
2 flakes garlic - chopped
½ tbsp oil
¼ tsp crushed fresh peppercorns (saboot kali mirch)
½ tsp salt, ½ tsp sugar
2 tsp mustard paste approx.

OTHER INGREDIENTS
2 slices pineapple - cut into 1" pieces
4-5 olives or cherries, optional
¾ cup carrots - cut into paper thin round slices (1 large carrot)
½ cup baby corns - cut into paper thin round slices
2-3 red radish - cut into slices or a tomato - cut into 8 pieces and pulp removed
1 capsicum - cut into ½" pieces
12-15 paper thin slices of unpeeled cucumber
4-5 lettuce leaves - torn into 1" pieces

MARINADE FOR THE VEGETABLES
½ cup vinegar, 1 cup ice cold water
lots of ice cubes, 1 tsp salt, 1 tsp sugar

1. Mix all ingredients of the mustard dressing till smooth. Keep in the refrigerator till serving time.
2. Mix vinegar with all the other ingredients of the marinade in a large bowl. Add carrots, baby corns, radish, capsicum, cucumber and lettuce. Keep in the fridge for 1-2 hours or till serving time.
3. At serving time, pick up the vegetables from the water marinade and put on a clean kitchen towel. Pat dry and keep in the serving bowl. Arrange 1-2 lettuce leaves on the sides.
4. Add pineapple pieces and olives or cherries. Mix.
5. Pour the mustard dressing over it and gently mix. The dressing should not be mixed too well. Serve immediately.

Broccoli Salad

Serves 4

1 small flower (125 gms) broccoli (hari gobhi) - cut into small sized florets
1 medium apple
1 tomato - cut into 4 pieces, remove seeds and chop into small pieces
1 capsicum - chop into small pieces
1 onion - chopped

DRESSING
¼ cup cream
¼ cup tomato sauce
1 tbsp lemon juice, 1 tbsp soya sauce
6-8 flakes of garlic
½-1 tsp sugar (depending on taste)
½ tsp salt, 1 tsp pepper powder
2 tbsp chopped coriander leaves
2 tbsp chopped mint leaves (poodina)

1. Cut broccoli into very small florets with long stalks.
2. Boil 2 cups water in a large pan. Add ¾ tsp salt and ½ tsp sugar to the water. Add broccoli pieces to the boiling water. Bring to a boil again. Drain immediately and rinse in cold water to prevent further cooking.

3. In a small mixer put all the ingredients of dressing. Churn well for 2 minutes. Keep dressing aside in the mixer itself.
4. Chop the apple alongwith the peel into very small pieces. In a bowl mix broccoli, apple, tomato, capsicum and onion.
5. Pour the prepared dressing on the vegetables and mix well. Check salt and pepper.

6. Transfer to a serving bowl. Chill in the fridge till serving time.
7. To serve, mix the salad well with two forks. Garnish with a tomato rose and fresh coriander or mint sprigs. Serve chilled.

Note: Instead of broccoli, cauliflower can be used. You can top the salad with some roasted almonds or walnuts also.

Thai Salad on Sticks

Tofu is an important ingredient in Thai cooking is a rich source of proteins for the vegetarians. You can use paneer instead.

Makes 6 Skewers

100 gm tofu or paneer - cubed to get 1½ " squares
6 baby corns, small sized - put in boiling water for 3 minutes and wipe dry
6 mushrooms - trim stalk and keep whole, 1 green capsicum - cut into 1" cubes
6 cherry tomatoes or 1 large, firm tomato cut into 8 pieces and pulp removed

MARINADE

½ tsp salt, ¼-½ tsp red chilli powder, 2 tsp brown sugar or gur
2 fresh red chillies - seeded and thinly sliced
3 tbsp coconut milk or 3 tbsp coconut milk powder (maggi) mixed with 2 tbsp milk
½ tsp soya sauce, 1" piece of ginger - grated
1 tsp lemon juice, 1 tsp brown or ¾ tsp regular sugar, 2 tsp cornflour
8-10 flakes garlic - crushed to a paste
½ tsp jeera powder (ground cumin), ½ tsp dhania powder

1. Boil 3 cups water in a pan, add babycorn and mushrooms in it. Boil for 2-3 minutes. Remove from fire, strain and refresh in cold water.
2. Mix all ingredients of marinade together. Add tofu or paneer, blanched baby corns, mushrooms and tomatoes. Keep covered for ½ hour or till serving time.
3. Thread a mushroom, then a baby corn, then a cherry tomato or regular tomato piece and lastly a paneer piece onto oiled wooden skewers. Leave behind the marinade. Keep aside.
4. Cook in a preheated oven at 180°C/350°F for 6-7 minutes. Baste (pour) with a spoon the remaining marinade on the sticks and cook for another 2-3 minutes. Serve.

How to Boil Pasta

(2 cups uncooked pasta will give 3½ cups boiled pasta)

To boil 2 cups pasta, boil 8 cups water with 1 tsp salt and 1 tbsp oil. Add pasta to boiling water. Stir to see that pasta is not sticking to the bottom of the pan. Boil, stirring occasionally, for about 7-8 minutes till pasta turns almost soft, but yet firm. Do not overcook. Remove from fire and leave pasta in hot water for 2-3 minutes. Strain. Leave for 5-7 minutes in the strainer for all the water to drain out. Spoon 1 tbsp olive oil on the cooked pasta to prevent it from sticking.

How to Boil Rice

(1 cup uncooked rice will give 1½-2 cups boiled rice)

Wash 1 cup rice with several changes of water till the water is clean. Keep aside. Boil 6 cups water with 1 tsp salt and 1 tbsp lemon juice in a deep pan. Add the rice to the boiling water. Boil for about 4-5 minutes till almost done. Remove from water. Strain through a big strainer or colander. Fluff with a fork to let the steam escape. Pour 2-3 cups tap water on the rice to arrest the heat otherwise sometimes the rice turns mushy. Leave rice in the strainer for 10-15 minutes. Spread the rice on a tray to turn dry.

How to Boil Noodles

(100 gm noodles will give 2½ cups boiled noodles)

To boil 100 gms of noodles, heat 4-5 cups of water in a pan with 1 tsp salt and 1 tbsp oil. Add noodles to boiling water. Boil for 1-2 minutes till slightly undercooked. Do not cook till soft. Remove from fire. Strain and refresh in cold water immediately. Let them be in the strainer for 10 minutes for all the water to drain out. Sprinkle 1 tsp oil on them and mix well. Spread noodles on a tray covered with a cloth napkin.

Rice & Corn Salad

Serves 4

MIX TOGETHER GENTLY

¾ cup rice (long grain basmati) or 1 cup boiled rice, see page 69
1 small cucumber (kheera) - washed well and chopped with the peel (1 cup)
1 cup tinned corn kernels
1 tbsp olive oil
1 red or green capsicum - chopped
4-5 black olives or jalapenos (optional) - sliced
½ tsp salt, ½ tsp pepper
½ tsp oregano
2 tbsp lemon juice

TEMPERING (CHOWNK/TADKA)

1 tbsp olive oil, ¼ tsp salt
1 onion - sliced
2-3 tbsp finely chopped parsley or basil or coriander
1 tbsp chopped walnuts (akhrot) or ¼ cup thickly grated fresh coconut

OTHER INGREDIENTS

2-3 cabbage leaves - whole, dipped in a bowl of water and put in the fridge

1. To boil rice, see page 69.
2. Chop cucumber with the peel. Keep aside.
3. To the rice, add all the ingredients written under rice. Mix well with a fork. Do not let the grains of rice break.
4. For tempering, heat oil in a non stick pan, add the onion and cook for 1 minute. Add all the other remaining ingredients. Stir for 1 minute. Remove from fire.
5. Pour this softened onion slices over the rice mixture. Mix lightly.
6. Transfer half of the salad to a serving bowl. Cut the stalk end of the cabbage leaves and pat dry on a clean kitchen towel. Arrange 2-3 cabbage leaves on the rice on any one side of the bowl such that they are about 1" above the level of the bowl. Now put the remaining salad.
7. Serve at room temperature or chill for 1 hour in the fridge.
Serve garnished with chopped basil or parsley, topped with a few walnuts.

Glass Noodle Veg Salad

Serves 6-8

3 cups glass noodles or rice vermicelli or thin white bean threads
8-10 french beans - chopped
100 gm baby corns - sliced diagonally thinly
1 large carrot - sliced diagonally thinly
1 spring onion chopped with greens (½ cup)

DRESSING

4 tbsp oil (sesame oil, preferably)
2 tbsp light soya sauce use less if using a dark soya sauce
1 tbsp vinegar
2 tbsp Worcestershire sauce
2 tbsp green chilli sauce, 2 tbsp red chilli sauce
2 tbsp tomato ketchup, 1 tsp crushed garlic, ¾ tsp salt, ½ tsp pepper

TO GARNISH

1 tbsp roasted peanuts (moongphali) - split into two by rolling with a rolling pin
(chakla-belan)

1. To boil glass noodles, heat 4 cups of water in a pan with 1 tsp salt. Add noodles to boiling water. Remove from fire. Leave in hot water for 2 minutes or till noodles are slightly soft. Strain and refresh in cold water immediately. Let them be in the strainer for 10 minutes for all the water to drain out.

2. Again boil 2 cups water with 1 tsp salt. Add thin, diagonal slices of carrots, baby corns and french beans. When the boil returns after a minute, remove from fire. Strain immediately and refresh by adding cold water. Leave the blanched vegetables in the strainer for 15 minutes for the water to drain out completely.

2. Mix all the ingredients of the dressing. Transfer noodles to a bowl and pour ½ of the dressing over the boiled noodles. Mix well and chill in the fridge for 30 minutes.

4. Add the leftover dressing, blanched vegetables and spring onions to the noodles. Mix well and chill till serving time.

5. At serving time, top with some roasted peanuts.

Roasted Pasta Salad

Picture on facing page   *Serves 4*

200 gm (2 cups) pasta - bows or spirals or penne pasta
2 large green peppers (capsicums) or 1 red & 1 green pepper
1 tbsp olive oil, preferably or any other cooking oil
2-3 tbsp cream or mayonnaise, 1 spring onion greens - sliced, to garnish

TOMATO DRESSING
2 tbsp olive oil, 4 flakes garlic - crushed and chopped
4 large tomatoes, 1 tbsp ready made tomato puree
2 tbsp tomato sauce, 1 tbsp vinegar, 1¼ tsp salt
1 tsp oregano, a pinch of sugar, 1 tsp red chilli flakes

1. To boil pasta, boil 8 cups water with 1 tsp salt and 1 tbsp oil. Add pasta to boiling water. Stir to see that pasta is not sticking to the bottom of the pan. Boil, stirring occasionally, for about 7-8 minutes till pasta turns almost soft, but yet firm. Do not overcook. Remove from fire and leave pasta in hot water for 2-3 minutes. Strain. Leave for 5-7 minutes in the strainer for all the water to drain out. Spoon 1 tbsp olive oil on the cooked pasta to prevent it from sticking. *Contd...*

2. Transfer boiled pasta to a bowl and pour 1 tbsp olive oil and cream or mayonnaise on it. Mix well. Keep aside.

3. Pierce a washed capsicum with a fork. Hold it directly on the gas flame. Roast it on all sides for 1-2 minutes till outer skin of capsicum gets black spots all around. Cool. Chop roasted capsicums into small pieces. Add to the pasta. Keep aside.

4. To prepare dressing, place the tomatoes in boiling water and boil for 2-3 minutes. Remove from water and cool. Peel the tomatoes and grind in a mixer to a smooth puree. Keep fresh tomato puree aside.

5. Heat 2 tbsp oil in a pan. Reduce heat and add garlic. Stir and add the fresh tomato puree.

6. Stir for 2-3 minutes and add the ready made tomato puree, tomato sauce, vinegar, salt, oregano, sugar and chilli flakes. Stir and add ½ cup water and give one boil. Simmer for 1-2 minutes. Check the seasoning and remove from heat. Cool slightly and pour over the pasta. Toss gently. Chill in the fridge till serving time. Garnish with spring onions.

◁ *Full Meal Pasta Salad : Recipe on page 78*

Full Meal Pasta Salad

Delicious salad, a hearty meal by itself.

Picture on page 76   *Serves 6-8*

1½ cups pasta (shell or elbow macaroni) - boiled to get 2 cups
1 apple - unpeeled cored cubed or diced & sprinkled with some lemon juice
6-8 green grapes - halved
6-8 black grapes - halved or 15 cherries
75 gm paneer - cut into ¼" cubes (see note)
10 almonds - blanched and halved
2 celery sticks - chopped (optional), juice of 1 lemon

DRESSING
4 tbsp cream (¼ cup)
½ cup curd - hung for 15 minutes and whipped till smooth
¼ cup cold milk, ½ tsp mustard powder
¾ tsp salt, ½ tsp black pepper, 1 tsp oregano

1. Boil 8 cups water with 1 tsp salt and 1 tsp oil. Add macaroni to boiling water. When it is almost done, remove from fire. Leave macaroni in hot water for only 4-5 minutes to get soft. Drain. Refresh in cold water. Cover and keep aside.

2. To prepare the dressing, beat the curd with milk, mustard powder, salt, pepper and oregano till smooth.

3. Add the cream to the curd mixture. Mix well. Keep the dressing covered in the refrigerator.

4. Place the boiled pasta or macaroni in a bowl. Add apples, grapes, almonds, paneer and celery. Add lemon juice. Mix well and refrigerate.

5. At serving time, add the dressing to the pasta mixture and mix gently with 2 forks. Transfer to a salad bowl or platter and garnish with lettuce leaves or cabbage leaves. Serve cold.

Variation:

You can use cheese shavings instead of paneer cubes. To make cheese shavings, chill the cheese in the freezer till really cold. Then peel the cheese with a peeler to get thin long strips or shavings. Cashewnuts can be used instead of almonds.

Green Papaya Salad

The popular Thai salad with a chilli-lemon dressing. Choose a hard, raw papaya with a white flesh. Even a slightly ripe papaya with an orangish flesh is not suitable for this salad. Add very little soya sauce.

Serves 4-6

3 cups grated hard, raw papaya (1 small kachcha papita), see note given below
1 tomato - cut into 4 pieces and deseeded, cut into strips
½ cup tender green beans (French beans or lobia or chawli) - sliced very finely
¼ cup roasted peanuts (moongphali)- crushed coarsely

DRESSING
1 tsp light Soya sauce, 3 tbsp lemon juice, 2 tbsp sugar
½ tsp red chilli flakes, ½ tsp salt, or to taste
2 tbsp finely chopped coriander

CRUSH TOGETHER
3-4 red or green chillies and 1 flake garlic

1. Crush together red or green chillies with garlic to a rough paste. Mix this paste with all the other ingredients of the dressing in a flat bowl.
2. Peel and grate papaya from the biggest holes into thick long shreds. Add chopped beans and tomatoes and papaya to the dressing in the flat dish. Mix well. Cover with a cling film and chill for at least one hour, so that the flavours penetrate.
3. To serve, mix in half the peanuts. Serve topped with rest of the roasted peanuts.

Note: For an authentic papaya salads, peel the papaya and cut into slices. Cut slices into juliennes (matchsticks). To make work simpler, I have grated the papaya. If using dark soya sauce, addd just a few drops to keep the colour bright.

Steamed Zucchini Salad

Zucchini is like the Indian tori, but it has a lighter & a softer peel.
So it tastes good along with the peel. If you want, you can substitute tori for
zucchini but remember to buy tender ones, but do peel them lightly.

Serves 4

2 zucchinis or tori - sliced diagonally into ¼" thick pieces without peeling
2 tomatoes - finely chopped, 1 tsp honey
2-3 tbsp finely chopped coriander leaves
3/4 tsp salt, or to taste, ½ tsp pepper
½ tsp bhuna jeera (roasted cumin) powder
1 tbsp lemon juice

1. Wash and cut zucchini into ¼" thick, slanting slices.
2. Put in a big colander (stainless strainer) and place strainer over a pan of boiling water. Cover strainer and steam the zucchini for 5 minutes.
3. Remove from fire. Pour ice cold water over it to refresh it. Leave in the strainer for 15 minutes to drain off all the water. Transfer to a bowl.
4. Add all the other ingredients and toss. Leave it for an hour. Serve chilled.

Honey Chilli Sprouts

Serves 4

3 cups (300 gm) moong sprouts or mixed sprouts
2 tsp honey, 2 tbsp lemon juice, 2 tsp soya sauce
½ tsp red chilli powder, ½ tsp salt
8-10 saboot kali mirch (peppercorns) - crushed
1 tomato - chopped finely, 1 green chilli - chopped finely
1½" piece ginger - finely grated (1 tbsp)

GARNISH

greens of 1 spring onion - finely chopped or 1 tbsp chopped coriander

1. Steam the sprouts by placing them on a large stainless steel strainer (colander) on a pan of boiling water for 5-6 minutes till slightly soft. Remove from heat. (See note).
2. Transfer sprouts to a bowl. Add all the other ingredients and toss well.
3. Garnish with some finely chopped spring onion greens or coriander.

Note: You can also steam the sprouts in a microwave. Wash sprouts. Put in a plastic (polythene) bag. Micro high for 3 minutes.

Cheesy Tomato Boats

Picture on facing page   *Serves 4*

2 firm big, longish tomatoes
50 gms paneer - grated (4 tbsp)
1 tbsp chopped coriander
1 tsp finely chopped onion, optional
½" piece of ginger - grated, 1 tsp lemon juice
3-4 saboot kali mirch (peppercorns) - crushed
¼ tsp salt, or to taste

TO GARNISH
a few olives, optional, some parsley or coriander

1. Cut a very thin slice from the top of each tomato. Scoop out the pulp from tomatoes with a knife or a scooper leaving the walls intact. Rub some salt inside and keep them inverted for a few minutes.
2. Gently mix grated paneer with all the other ingredients.
3. Stuff into the tomato shells and press well. Cut each tomato into 4 pieces lengthwise, with a sharp knife.
4. Garnish each boat with a slice of olive & a coriander or parsley leaf.

Moong Anaarkali Salad

Serves 4   *Picture on opposite page*

2 cups moong sprouts
1 cup annar ke daane (fresh pomegranate)
1 potato - boiled & chopped
½ cup chopped cucumber alongwith peel (kheera)
1 tbsp roasted moongphali (peanuts) - coarsely ground
1 green chilli - remove seeds and chop finely
½ cup curd, 1 tsp salt
¼ tsp red chilli powder or pepper to taste, 1 tsp vinegar

1. Put moong sprouts in a big colander (stainless steel strainer) and place the strainer over a pan of boiling water. Cover the strainer and steam the sprouts for 5 minutes. Remove from fire.
2. In a bowl beat curd. Add salt, red chilli powder or pepper and vinegar.
3. Add moong sprouts, annar, potato, cucumber, peanuts, green chilli and mix well. Transfer to a serving dish. Garnish with anaar ke dane. Serve chilled.

Chat-Pata Protein Salad

Serves 6

½ cup kabuli channa (chick peas) - soaked overnight
½ cup rajmah (kidney beans) - soaked overnight
½ cup moong sprouts
1 capsicum - cut into half and then into thin rings
1 tomato - cut into half and then into round slices
1 onion - cut into half and then into thin rings
½ or a small cucumber (kheera) - cut into thin slices

DRESSING
1 tsp salt
1 tsp pepper
1 tsp ajwain (carom seeds)
1 tsp amchoor (dry mango powder)
a few basil or tulsi leaves
4 tsp vinegar or lemon juice
2 tsp oil

1. Soak rajmah and channas together. Next morning discard water. Add 1 tsp salt and pressure cook with 2 cups water to give 2 whistles. Keep on low flame for 10 minutes. When the pressure drops, strain the rajmah and channas and discard the water. Keep aside.

2. Steam the moong sprouts by placing them on a strainer or colander over a pan of boiling water for 3-4 minutes. Cover the colander while steaming. Remove from fire and keep aside.

3. Put all the dressing ingredients in a bottle and tightly close the cap. Shake vigorously to mix well. Keep aside.

4. Keep the cooked rajmah, channas, sprouts, capsicum, onion, tomato and cucumber in a large bowl. Chill.

5. An hour before serving, pour the dressing over and toss well with two forks to mix well. Serve.

Baked Tomato Cups

Serves 6

6 tomatoes - medium sized, even shaped and firm
2 tbsp channa dal
100 gms paneer (of toned milk) - grated
1 small apple - peeled and finely chopped
1 tsp mustard paste, ½ tsp salt
8-10 peppercorns - crushed
a few coriander leaves

1. Boil channa dal in some water with ½ tsp salt. Cook till just done. Strain and keep aside.
2. Cut tomatoes from top. Scoop the pulp. If you wish, rub a pinch of salt inside the hollow tomatoes. Keep them inverted on a plate.
3. Mix dal, paneer & apple. Add mustard paste, salt & pepper to taste.
4. Fill the mixture in tomatoes. To make the tomatoes stand upright, cut a thin slice from the base of the tomatoes.
5. At serving time, bake at 200°C for 12-15 minutes till soft but firm.
6. Garnish each with a coriander leaf. Serve on a bed of cabbage leaves.

Vegetable Sticks with Dip

Serves 6

home made paneer prepared from ½ kg of toned milk
1 cup curd - hang for ½ hour, 2-3 flakes garlic
2 tbsp chopped coriander leaves
a pinch of sugar, juice of 1 lemon
½ tsp salt, ½ tsp pepper
½ onion - very finely chopped

VEGETABLE STICKS
carrot, tomato, radish (mooli), cucumber (with the peel)

1. In a blender, mix paneer, curd, garlic, coriander leaves, sugar, lemon juice, salt and pepper to a paste. Mix well.
2. Add very finely chopped onion. Mix well.
3. Cut the carrot, tomato, radish and cucumber (with the peel) longitudinally into long fingers or sticks.
4. Arrange the salad in a plate with the dip in the centre.

Fruity Salad in Orange Dressing

Serves 4

½ cup cabbage - chopped
½ cup carrot - chopped
¼ cup onion - chopped
½ cup tomatoes - chopped
½ cup grapes or strawberries - halved or chopped
½ cup orange segments (pieces)

ORANGE DRESSING
1 tbsp oil
¼ cup orange juice (fresh or ready made)
1 tsp lemon juice
2-3 flakes garlic - crushed, ½ tsp oregano
½ tsp salt and pepper, or to taste

1. Mix all fruits and vegetables in a large bowl. Chill in the fridge till serving time.
2. Mix all ingredients of the orange dressing in a bottle. Close cap and shake well to mix. Keep aside.
3. An hour before serving, pour the dressing over the fruit and vegetable mixture in the bowl.
4. Toss lightly with two forks. Add more salt and pepper if desired.
5. Refrigerate till serving time.

Broccoli & Bean Salad in Mustard Dressing

Serves 4

VEGETABLES
100 gm (20-25) tender French beans
1 small (250 gm) broccoli (hari gobhi)
1 tomato or 3-4 strawberries

MUSTARD DRESSING
2 tsp mustard paste
½ tsp peppercorns - crushed
½ tsp salt
juice of 1 large lemon (2½-3 tbsp)
10-15 flakes garlic - sliced finely

1. Mix all ingredients of the dressing together in a small bowl.
2. Thread beans and cut into 1½" long pieces.
3. Cut broccoli into medium florets with a little stalk.
4. Cut strawberries or tomato lengthwise into slices. Remove pulp from tomatoes.
5. Boil 4-5 cups water with 2 tsp salt and 2 tsp sugar.
6. Add beans to the boiling water. As soon as the boil returns, keep the beans boiling for 1 minute.
7. Add broccoli. Remove from fire. Leave vegetables in hot water for 2 minutes.
8. Strain the vegetables. Refresh by taking them out of cold water. Leave in the strainer to drain out all the water.
9. Pat dry the vegetables on a cloth napkin and transfer them to a mixing bowl.
10. Add the sliced tomatoes or strawberries.
11. Add the dressing to the vegetables. Toss to mix well. Serve cold.

Dieter's Creamy Salad

Serves 6

2½ cups toned milk, ½ cup curd or juice of ½ lemon - to curdle milk
1 cup thick curd - hang for ½ hour, 2 tsp sugar
few drops of tabasco sauce or ½ tsp mustard paste
½ carrot - finely cubed and boiled till crisp tender
½ capsicum - cut into thin strips, ½ cup grapes -halved
1 apple - chopped without peeling, ½ cup chopped cucumber (kheera)

1. Boil milk. Reduce flame and add curd or lemon juice to curdle the milk. As soon as the milk curdles, remove from flame and strain through a muslin cloth. Leave paneer in the cloth for at least ½ hour till the water (whey) gets drained.
2. Blend paneer, curd, sugar and tabasco or mustard in a mixer.
3. Remove from mixer to a bowl. Add salt and pepper. Mix most of the fruits and vegetables in the curd-paneer mixture, keeping aside some for garnishing. Transfer to a serving bowl. Chill. Serve.

Potato Salad

Serves 4

Potatoes unless fried are not fattening at all! They are rich in carbohydrates which keep you full for a long time.

250 gms baby potatoes - boiled and peeled
½ cup thick curd - whipped till smooth
½ tsp salt
½ tsp peppercorns - crushed, ½ tsp mustard paste
2 tbsp mint leaves (finely chopped)
½ tsp soya sauce, 3/4 tsp chilli sauce

1. Boil the baby potatoes. Peel them.
2. In a bowl beat the curd well till smooth.
3. To the curd add all other ingredients, except the boiled potatoes. Mix well.
4. Add the boiled potatoes. Mix gently and transfer to a serving dish.
5. Garnish with fresh mint. Serve.

Salad Dressings

Dressings add colour, flavour, improve palatability and appearance and are a means of combining ingredients. These are general types of salad dressings which can used with any salads :

Mayonnaise (with eggs)

Makes 1½ cups

2 eggs, ½ tsp salt, ½ tsp pepper
1 tsp mustard powder, 2 tsp sugar, 1 tbsp vinegar, 1 tbsp lemon juice
1½ cups cooking oil (use absolutely clean oil should be unused)

1. Break eggs into the blender of your mixer. Add salt, pepper, sugar, mustard and vinegar to the eggs. Churn for a few seconds to blend all ingredients.
2. Keeping blender on, add oil slowly spoonful by spoonful, churning continuously.
3. Keep adding oil gradually, till the sauce starts to thicken. Once the sauce thickens slightly, keeping the blender on, pour oil in a thin stream from the cup directly in larger quantities. Churn till all the oil is used

and a thick mayonnaise is ready.
4. Add lemon juice. Churn once more. Remove from mixer to a bowl. Chill for 2 hours before use.

Eggless Mayonnaise

Serving 1 cup

3 tbsp oil, 2 tbsp flour (maida)
½ cup cold milk
salt, pepper to taste, 1 tsp lemon juice
50 gm (¼ cup) cream
¼ tsp salt, ½ tsp mustard powder
¼ tsp pepper powder, 1 tsp powdered sugar

1. Heat oil in a small heavy bottomed pan. Add flour. Reduce flame and stir for a minute. Add milk, stirring continuously. Boil. Cook till a thick white sauce is ready.
2. Whip white sauce after it cools to room temperature. Add lemon juice, salt, mustard powder, pepper and sugar. Gently mix in cream. Keep in the fridge.

FRENCH OR VINAIGRETTE DRESSING (MAKES ½ CUP)
2 tbsp vinegar, ½ cup olive or regular oil
½ tsp French mustard or mustard powder, 1 tsp salt
½ tsp powdered sugar ½ tsp pepper powder, 2 tsp lemon juice

1. Put all ingredients in a bottle with a tight fitting lid. Shake vigorously. Refrigerate until needed. Shake again before use.

Note: Excess French dressing will make green leafy vegetables flabby.

CURD DRESSING (MAKES 1¼ CUP)
1 cup curd - lightly beaten, 4 tbsp olive oil, 2 tbsp vinegar
1 tsp mustard, ½ tsp salt, ¼ tsp sugar, ¼ tsp pepper
¼ cup finely chopped coriander or parsley

1. Microwave coriander or parsley in some water for 2- 3 minutes. Remove. Drain.
2. Place all the ingredients in a bowl and mix well with a balloon whisk. Chill and serve.

CREAM DRESSING (MAKES 1½ CUPS)
1 cup cream - beaten, ½ cup olive oil, 2 tbsp vinegar, 1 tsp mustard
½ tsp salt,¼ tsp sugar, ¼ tsp chilli powder
¼ tsp black pepper, 1 tsp sesame seeds (til)

1. Roast til on a tawa till golden.
2. Place all the ingredients in a bottle and shake well.

SIMPLE VEGETABLE CUTTING

Shredding: to cut into thin, long pieces
The vegetables are cut into thin, strips or shreds. Spinach, lettuce, cabbage are all shredded. Carrot can be grated on the big holes of a grater to get shredded carrot.

Jullienes: cut into thin match stick pieces : The vegetables are cut into thin slices lengthwise. The slices are stacked together and cut lengthwise to get thin match sticks. Carrots and cucumber jullienes look good.

Slicing: to cut completely through the vegetable to get slices : The vegetables are cut into thin slices. The thickness depends on what is specified in each individual recipe. Tomatoes, carrots, mushrooms, onions etc. are sliced in quite a few recipes.

Tomato pieces without pulp : Cut a firm tomato into 4 pieces, lengthwise. Remove pulp from each piece. Now cut the big piece into smaller pieces or strips.

Chopping: to cut into small pieces : The vegetable is cut into small pieces. Holding on to the vegetable firmly, cut the vegetable lengthwise into slices and then holding on firmly, give the sliced vegetable a quick turn at a right angle. Now cut the sliced vegetable again into slices which will result in finely  chopped pieces. Onions and tomatoes are usually chopped in the recipes.

Diagonal slices: to cut vegetable slices in a slanting manner : The vegetables are cut into thin slices in a slanting manner in such a way that there are more exposed surfaces. Vegetables such as asparagus, carrots, celery or French beans are usually diagonally sliced.

Rings and Half Rings: to cut vegetables widthwise into rounds : Vegetables like onions or capsicums are cut widthwise to get rounds. The onion slices are then separated to give full rings. For half rings, cut the vegetables first into half and then cut widthwise to get half rings. When opened the half rings look like thin strips of onion and can be used as shredded onion also.

Crispy Spinach with Feta : Recipe on page 26 ➢

$\mathcal{N}ita\ \mathcal{M}ehta's$ BEST SELLERS (Vegetarian)